An Epistle on the Two Mountains
of Faith & Feeling

Titles in the Series
Letters to the Devoted Follower of Christ

(in the order in which they were written)

AN EPISTLE TO THE MISERABLE
AN EPISTLE TO THE MODERATELY MISERABLE
AN EPISTLE ON JUDGMENT
ON THE TRIPARTITE NATURE OF MAN
AN EPISTLE ON MERCY
AN EPISTLE ON EXPECTATION
ON THE TWO MOUNTAINS OF FAITH & FEELING

AN EPISTLE ON
THE TWO MOUNTAINS OF
FAITH & FEELING

By

A Little Anchor of the Church

Series Dedication

For those who actually want
to walk the narrow Way

AN EPISTLE ON
THE TWO MOUNTAINS
OF FAITH & FEELING

Health, healing, and happiness to you, my dear friend in Christ, that you may be fully fit to serve in the Kingdom of God, as you desire. All praise, glory, and honor to the One Who alone is worthy of such adoration. To His Kingdom and the increase of His government and peace there shall be no end, amen.

You have asked for more details regarding the two mountains of faith and feeling I often mention in my letters. From the very start, let it be that clear I am not saying one is good and one is bad. They both have a place in a balanced life, as they did for Christ our Lord. Yet especially in hours of crisis, it is good to keep strong boundaries around the place where the soul lives, and around the larger expanse of land wherein the soul moves about, journeys, or just travels from place to place. This is common sense. We tend to lose sight, I believe, of what God considers part of a common life for us — *common* being commonplace and universal for His children.

God wishes a basic standard of life to be available to His followers at all times — and His basic standard is much higher than we typically settle for. We settle for being overrun (as though allowing lawbreakers to overrun us is somehow Christian*). But

---

* There is a significant difference between receiving a wrong to oneself and choosing how to retaliate, as Jesus was teaching in Matthew 5:38-39, and in defending one's borders for the defense of family and livelihood. Consider also what Jesus told His disciples in Luke 22:36. Our retaliation is to be limited according to the parameters of the Old Law; and under the New Law of Christ, we are not required to demand even what is just. We can choose to respond or not for ourself; but for the sake of the Church, or the children, or other innocents,

God would have our lives be free of violence, whether physically, emotionally, morally, or spiritually. This requires strong boundaries, and these boundaries are as important in the struggle between faith and feeling as they are anywhere else.

To reply to another of your comments — I desire that you not think of me as your teacher. I do not aspire to fill such an office, as though I might be thought of as one who sought to exercise authority over my fellow souls. We have all sinned and fallen far below the standard God originally set for Man. I do not believe we need to feel ever remorseful, but I do believe it is humble-ness that takes a soul further into the great Sea of God than anything else except for love. I seek to remain in a place of abase-ment—not seeking new experiences of such, but to remain in the low place in which my soul was tried for many years. Perhaps if I labor in this way, I will avoid new trials that would bring me low,

---

we are not required to surrender them to evil entities who seek to do them harm.

because I already hold a low place. It is my desire to help if I can, that others may not have to bear the discipline I myself did. God does not design abasement for us; but He may have to leave us to it if we will not be moved by any better teaching aid. If I can offer you any useful spiritual counsel, well and good. But consider anything worthwhile to be taught to you by God's Spirit, not mine.

The descriptions I give of the interior land — you do not have to draw upon them for your meditations exactly as I describe them. If there are analogies you believe are better suited to the truths you are laboring to process, use them instead. I do not offer these things as the only spiritual interpretations that can be made, or the last word on any of these subjects. I use them to paint some pictures of that vast interior country. I do not wish you to conclude that the Holy Spirit ought to limit Himself to these I have given. Rather, I encourage you to begin to paint your own pictures in your contemplations of God and His spiritual Kingdom, all the while asking the Holy Spirit to consecrate your imagination. The abiding principle is simply this: they must not counter what has been revealed in God's Word. The willing soul will respect this divine boundary. That our contemplations may have more details than things dealt with in Scripture is acceptable. God has no issue with this, as long as our souls strive to remain pure. He *encourages* such contemplations, desiring that we make use of any good thing that can aid us in our understanding. In a similar manner in which a child approaches its guardian and confesses, "I've been thinking about something," and the guardian finds this touching and amusing, so does the Father in Heaven with His children who contemplate matters almost beyond their ken. He is far from offended by our simplistic contemplations, as long as they do not dishonor the standard He has set for us.

Regarding this standard, it is written that "whatsoever things are true, whatsoever things are honest, whatsoever things are just, whatsoever things are pure, whatsoever things are lovely, whatsoever things are of good report; if there be any virtue, and if there be any praise, think on these things."[*] We can hardly consider ourselves devoted followers of Christ if we do not adhere to principles such as this—followers, yes, but devoted followers, no.

If in any way our contemplations do not encourage virtue, we need to redirect them. And when there are voices which are purposely trying to feed your soul not just things which encourage vice, but things which intend to manipulate, step away whenever you can until they are out of earshot (for apart from the deceiving demonic, even men who call themselves persons of good will are tempted to manipulate the masses as soon as they hold places of influence if they are not kept protectively within the boundaries of His spiritual leading). The voices of culture bombard us at every step, so find a small place where you can restore your quiet as need be. Give it a few personal touches, and do what you can to

---

make it comfortable to you so that you will want to go there often.

WE have been speaking of two great mountains in the spiritual life — those of Faith and Feeling. Again, I do not wish to give the impression that matters of Faith vs. Feeling must be looked at in just this way. These likenesses are given simply to aid in the expression of the truths involved. Remember that like a photograph, likenesses are but the capturing of an instant's view; and God's Kingdom is ever shifting, ever adjusting to the new growth we bring to it. Its principles, the laws upon which it works, remain the same. But our vantage points change, and we see things in different lights. So our contemplations shift in response to these new perspectives. It is good to hold to our contemplations lightly, so that when something more useful to another season of life comes along, the mental transition is easy.

A foundational standard of living is applicable to all souls; a higher standard is required of Christ-followers — not because we can lose our salvation if (when) we do not perform as well as the next person. We do not lose that unless we fully renounce it (though some persons who profess to be followers may have never really received Christ and so never had salvation). A higher standard for the Christ-follower than for human souls in general is because the Truth of God has been revealed to the followers[*] — or rather, the Gate[†] of this Truth, both of which are Jesus Christ our Lord.

Passage through the Gate is free; how far the soul travels into the Kingdom of God — His Life, His Truth, His Way, etc. — is up to each soul. We can receive Him as the Gate, and hover about this entrance to the Land of Truth, or we can embark on a journey deeper into It across a vast and beautiful

---

[*] Matthew 13:10-11—"And the disciples came, and said unto Him, Why speakest Thou unto them in parables? He answered and said unto them, Because it is given unto you to know the mysteries of the kingdom of heaven, but to them it is not given." I speak on the need for parables further in this letter.
[†] John 10:7—"Then said Jesus unto them again, Verily, verily, I say unto you, I am the door of the sheep."

country. Jesus is the start of it all and the end, the first Word and the Last, the Alpha and the Omega.* He is our Way of Salvation,† and He is our communion with God the Father,‡ and eventually the everlasting relationship with God will be consummated through Him.§ This is why we say He is our answer for everything—because we embark on the spiritual journey by passing through this narrow Gate, but then the vista opens to a broad and spacious place.** All this is in the spiritual, as we say, *in Christ.*

---

* Revelation 22:13—"I am Alpha and Omega, the beginning and the end, the first and the last."

† John 14:6—"Jesus saith unto him, I am the way, the truth, and the life: no man cometh unto the Father, but by Me."

‡ John 17:26—"And I have declared unto them Thy name, and will declare it: that the love wherewith Thou hast loved Me may be in them, and I in them."

§ Revelation 19:9—"Then [the angel] said to me, Write this down: Blessed (happy, to be envied) are those who are summoned (invited, called) to the marriage supper of the Lamb. And he said to me [further], These are the true words (the genuine and exact declarations) of God" (AMPC).

** Psalm 18:19—"He brought me forth also into a large place; He delivered me, because He delighted in me."

God never forces or coerces us to journey further into the Christ-land, and many choose to build houses on the sand near the Gate instead of on the Great Rock further in, the Mountain of our Faith. But to pass through the Gate at all means relinquishing citizenship in the kingdom of death and receiving it in the Kingdom of Light, thus making souls who possess such new citizenship subordinate to the law of this new land. Souls live by a higher law once they pass through that Gate, and that's just how it is. If they fail to uphold the integrity this standard requires, God is not going to kick them out of the Kingdom. (Spiritually speaking they are removing themselves for a time to visit the kingdom of darkness to pursue some act that falls short of the standard of the glory of God for our lives. All God says is, "If you want to do such things, it is your right to do so, but you can't do them Here in My Kingdom.") But He can't take and place them in high places of authority in His Kingdom, especially if they won't move from their place just beside the Gate. Or if they have for a time gained a high place without committing to walking the higher standard, you will see in time that this was not a true spiritual promotion and that they no longer possess what it appeared they would always have. Not only did they not earn such a promotion by receiving a true calling, they also disqualified themselves by continuing in sin. Some are also unqualified to rule because they have not experienced the matters involved. It is like expecting to get a high-level managerial promotion in a company when you've only worked as a receptionist in the front office.

This promotion to a higher standard has to do with our eternal reward, which many make light of because they have so little understanding of Heaven and eternal life. This higher standard is also for the enablement of fulfilling the purposes for which spirits are sent into this earth. The higher the purpose, the higher the standard to which a soul must hold fast. But it is not necessarily true that the higher the purpose, the greater the reward. Sometimes the lowest, most ostracized soul will receive a superabundant reward once it returns Home because it persevered in its faith despite what was for it, the most oppressive conditions that could exist for that soul. We must remind ourselves that God's equations are far too complex for Man to compute. Some things must be left to Him, and for our part we follow after Christ the best we can, trusting always in the Blood of Jesus which was mercifully shed for our redemption.

The basest of sinners can meet the standard for soul-salvation, which is simply to receive Jesus in humble sincerity as their Saviour because they freely acknowledge there is no other means by which they can be saved or to fully atone for their sins. Many persons do not look forward to Heaven because they picture us sitting around forever and mostly *feeling* happy. Maybe there'll be some singing; but after the first flush of reunion with those who passed on ahead of us, they wonder how we won't go mad with boredom without a little evil to battle now and again. The matter of reward is not of much interest to them. But God never minces words. He has spoken of our heavenly reward, so it must be important to Him that we comprehend better what we are laboring toward here. (And there will be ever so much more to do than sitting around feeling happy.) Again, taking likenesses helps many souls better suss out what this life is all about, both in the vital importance of believing on Jesus of Nazareth as Saviour and Lord, and in respecting that how we live on earth is extremely important to God. Respecting something does not necessitate always understanding it. If you feel you do better without such likenesses, then gloss over them and simply adhere to the best of your ability to the commands we have been given. But many are helped by them, which is why Jesus so often utilized them.

I HAVE likened these two disparate realms of Faith and Feeling as two large mountains, between which lies a great crevasse known as the Valley of Fact. Here are some thoughts regarding the Valley of Fact which lies between these two mountains, because

I have to this point commented less on this than on the others, and because it seems a good place to start:

The Valley of Fact is synonymous with the Word of God, or God's Truth, both for Man in general and for our personal walks as followers of Christ. For Man in general our Truth is the eternal Word of God which has set a standard of life for all men and women. It is the common law by which God evaluates our lives. He set it down for us, and so, being LORD, He has a right to demand we obey it.* For individual followers

---

* God entrusted this common law (particularly, the Ten Commandments) to Israel (Romans 3:1-2), which He drew out from among the nations of the earth to be His illustrative nation for His ways and to keep the line intact from which the Messiah would be born. If we wonder whether Jesus was really sent by God, well, those who researched His life believed there was a link from Him all the way back to God (Luke 3:23-38, and the belief Jesus was the Messiah sent by God—the One to save the people from their sins—is consistent in all four accounts of the Gospel message). Consider Romans 4:16, which teaches that the salvation entrusted to the Jews is free for any who will believe, which was not always readily apparent to the disciples in the Gospel accounts, who interpreted Jesus as being their nation's Saviour throughout His earthly ministry. Through the apostle Paul, a vessel of the Lord's mighty intellect, the universal nature of Christ's mission was made clearer. The Jews served as priests for the faith entrusted to

14

of Christ, this Truth is also the application of the principles embedded in the Word for our personal situation and temperament. This Word births more in our lives as we walk the Path of Christ, because we have honored Him by placing our faith in His Beloved Son; therefore He also honors us with many blessings, the fruit of our faith.

This valley between the Mounts of Faith and Feeling is not wrong, as though it might be simply because it is not on either of the mountains. -or as though it somehow becomes a wrong place to be when we walk on the lower paths of spiritual communion with God. Yet the lower paths are not necessarily baser forms of communion with God: they are instead the *basics* of our faith. So it is good to traverse them regularly. They begin to lose their value only when souls refuse to climb any higher. Some feel

---

them among the nations of the earth (or God planned for them to do so; Exodus 19:6—"And you shall be to Me a kingdom of priests, a holy nation [consecrated, set apart to the worship of God]" (AMPC). This responsibility was subsequently transferred to the Church—not to exclude the Jews thereafter, but to incorporate Gentiles (Revelation 1:6 & Romans 11:17-24).

they do well to build their spiritual home a little ways up the Mount of Faith — thereby not dwelling in the Valley itself — but it is so close to the sandy floor that they are hardly protected from anything that might strike lowlands.

In the Valley there are shadows, nestled as it is between those two massive boulders, because until the last enemy is defeated — death* — there will always be a shadow of it in the reality of Man's existence. It is not that it can touch us in the spiritual realm, but we can still see the *shadow* of it. This is why the Word states, "Yea, though I walk through the valley of the shadow of death, I will fear no evil."†

It is difficult to expound on every point in every letter — here as to the truth of why God made a way for death not to touch us. I will speak more on this in another letter, as I have tried to address other questions such as this for you. One of the main points is that we must take hold of this and all

---

* I Corinthians 15:26—"The last enemy that shall be destroyed is death."
† Psalm 23:4

God's truths by faith, so until you understand why things are the way they are, just continue to nurture sincere trust that the Lord has it all in hand. There are many other facts to our existence too.

There is the fact of God's mercy: "The LORD is merciful and gracious, slow to anger, and plenteous in mercy."* Long ago, God's own people testified to this while readying themselves for battle: "Praise the LORD; for His mercy endureth for ever."†

There is the fact of God's willingness to bless. For did He not command blessings upon the poor in spirit, those who mourn, the humble and meek, the hungry and thirsty for righteousness, the merciful, the pure in heart, the peacemakers, the persecuted and reviled for righteousness?‡

There is the fact of the Atoning Sacrifice, the full and free conciliation for our sins: "Herein is love, not that we loved God, but

---

* Psalm 103:8

† II Chronicles 20:21

‡ Matthew 5:3-11; but again we must lay claim to the promises of God if we hope to receive the blessings of them. To have we must ask (James 4:2).

that He loved us, and sent His Son to be the propitiation for our sins."*

There is the fact of the overcoming nature in Christ: "In all these things we are more than conquerors through Him that loved us."†

There is the fact that at times the battle is the LORD's, not ours. [Soul sighs in relief.] "Be not afraid nor dismayed by reason of this great multitude; for the battle is not yours, but God's."‡

There is the fact of God's eternal remembrance of us: "Behold, I have graven thee upon the palms of My hands; thy walls are continually before Me."§

And on and on and on.

The Valley of Fact is where we begin. It was never intended to be our end. Even though reconciliation with God requires faith, the soul must exercise that faith based

---

* I John 4:10

† Romans 8:37

‡ II Chronicles 20:15. This is also what Moses told the people at the Red Sea when the Egyptians were running them down; see Exodus 14:14.

§ Isaiah 49:16

upon the truth of our need for a Saviour — faith and truth are inextricably linked. So our entrance into the Kingdom at the Valley of Fact serves as a beginning and a buffer between the two mountains, and someday we will be free to linger there as long as we will, no longer dominated by feeling and no longer requiring strong boundaries to guard a hard-won faith; we will have the evidence of the unseen, and everything will be as it should be.

Also, the lay of the land will take on much more varied contours, once we are no longer bound by earthly restrictions. There is much even seasoned seers* do not view at

---

* *Seers* are those who actually see the spiritual realm as it exists, or they see something in the present or past or future, not in symbolic vision but as it happened or will happen—though how much they see seems to be according to their faith. That is, if they expect to see little, they will perceive only a portion of any given vision; and if much, they will perceive in greater detail. There seems to be less of the symbolic going on than occurs in prophetic visions. This perhaps is because in many prophetic visions symbolism is heavily used to convey likenesses for us so that we better comprehend a spiritual situation. Such revelations are not dependent on, nor necessarily involve, what is going on in actuality in Heaven or elsewhere (which are the sights seers are often given). Rules of thumb: do not put God in a box, and He can and does place on some persons more than

present, for God does not reveal the whole of His Kingdom in Heaven to any mortal. We each see in part.* So there are no recriminations for seeing in part rather than in whole; seeing in part conforms to our present existence until the spirit is fully translated into Heaven. We are to labor to continue to see, hear, and comprehend what we are being taught, but God does not expect us to know or to understand everything. It is conceited to believe it has been appointed to our self to be a vessel which can know more than any other. Just make an effort to continue to grow in Christ, and the Father will be pleased. He will reveal to

---

one calling. E.g., one can be both a seer and a prophetic voice, just as one can be both apostle and prophet. It is similar to someone being both an artist and a musician.
* I Corinthians 13:12—"For now we are looking in a mirror that gives only a dim (blurred) reflection [of reality as in a riddle or enigma], but then [when perfection comes] we shall see in reality and face to face! Now I know in part (imperfectly), but then I shall know and understand fully and clearly, even in the same manner as I have been fully and clearly known and understood [by God]" (AMPC). It is not as much that God restricts our vision but that we fail to perceive everything that is to be seen. The imperfect will someday be swallowed up in perfection.

you what you personally need to know to keep climbing the Mountain of Faith.

Every time we leave the Mountain of Faith to visit the Mountain of Feeling, we must cross through the Valley of Fact. We can be intellectually and spiritually oblivious to our surroundings, or we can sleep throughout our travels, thus missing many words of truth God was making available to us. But we must pass through it regardless. It is the lay of the spiritual land. Why? Because Faith and Feeling are separate domains.

I am in no way saying that when we live on the Mount of Faith we ought to be without feeling or that feeling is inaccessible to us on the Mount of Faith. This is not what I mean at all. One can have faith and feel concurrently whether one is on the Mount of Faith or the Mount of Feeling. They are both part of our quantum reality in a sense. Can you point to any place in the Gospel accounts that demonstrate our Example, Jesus, was without feeling or taught us to aspire to be so? I do not believe you can. Neither can you point to a place in the accounts where Jesus, feeling deeply, was not also ultimately ruled by His faith in the Father.

It is the rock on which we establish our spiritual life that is the vital point here. It is the ruling domain that is in question — the domain ruled by Faith, or the domain ruled by Feeling. It is the choice of where to build our spiritual structure — that place from which we live and where we go when we want to escape the outside elements. If a soul wishes to build its structure in the domain of Feeling — feeling for God, for family, friends, the unsaved, the poor, etc. — it is free to do so. Both mountains are available to believers AFTER they pass through the Gate, as is the sandy floor of the valley. (Therefore all is of the Kingdom.) One is not good and the other evil. It is, rather, a matter of whether we will choose between something better and the best of what God fashioned for His children's lives. He never forces us to accept the best but always gives us choices.

The Lord taught us something about this in one of His parables, particularly regarding building on sand vs. rock: "Therefore whosoever heareth these sayings of Mine, and doeth them, I will liken him unto a wise man, which built his house upon a rock: and the rain descended, and the floods came, and the winds blew, and beat upon that house; and it fell not: for it was founded upon a rock. And every one that heareth these sayings of Mine, and doeth them not, shall be likened unto a foolish man, which built his house upon the sand: and the rain descended, and the floods came, and the winds blew, and beat upon that house; and it fell: and great was the fall of it."*

Haven't most of us known many sincere but erring believers who demonstrated they did not build on the Rock?

The sandy ground is for the comfort of those who are traversing the inner land during sunny conditions. When the rain pours down and beats upon sand and rock (which it does from time to time in the likeness of the spiritual Kingdom because

---

* Matthew 7:24-27

people *will* persist in trying to bring things into the Kingdom that God has to later wash away), I want to be in my little spiritual home on the Mount of Faith, not traveling about in a storm. Just as feeling is not wrong in its place, neither should we conclude God did not create sand for good purposes. Yet it is not the place to build upon.

We at first conclude this teaching must relate to souls outside the Kingdom because those in the Kingdom are most certainly protected. Aren't they? I would like to answer unequivocally in the affirmative to this question, but I cannot. For the truth of the matter as I see it, is that there are still dangers to the saved in the Kingdom. Why? –because the soul is transformed into the Christ-mettle in increments. It is not immediately made of the sterner stuff. So the Rock may be rolling on a mission — perhaps to provide much-needed water from which people in drought-afflicted lands can drink, as occurred in the wilderness,* or to bowl over in judgment or to establish the Mountain of the Dominion of Christ in the earth† — and the foolish soul (too filled with self and too ready to be prominently placed in the Path) can be in danger of being run over.

The more the soul submits itself to the transformative process, the less vulnerable it becomes to dangers, even dangers within the Kingdom. In one sense there are no dangers, for the soul cannot be damaged irrevocably as long as it does not renounce Christ. But it can be damaged insofar as its reward is concerned, or insofar as its earthly purposes are concerned (which in

---

* Exodus 17:5-6—"And the LORD said unto Moses, Go on before the people, and take with thee of the elders of Israel; and thy rod, wherewith thou smotest the river, take in thine hand, and go. Behold, I will stand before thee there upon the rock in Horeb; and thou shalt smite the rock, and there shall come water out of it, that the people may drink. And Moses did so in the sight of the elders of Israel."

† Daniel 2:35, 44-45—"Then was the iron, the clay, the brass, the silver, and the gold, broken to pieces together, and became like the chaff of the summer threshing-floors; and the wind carried them away, that no place was found for them: and the stone that smote the image became a great mountain, and filled the whole earth."

turn are attached to its eternal reward). The inner man can grow and become strong in Christ, or it can remain small and feeble, thus making it vulnerable to poor choices because it is tired and overtasked, trying to keep up in a land designed for those who are strong and courageous and capable of great things. On the sand is a pleasant place to be, where the water and sand are warm and refreshing, so those less fit for mountain-climbing naturally wish to settle here. Many souls do not build on sandy ground because they are purposely trying to be obstinate. They honestly feel, if only in some vague way, that they are not fit for making the treks up into the high ground. But I cannot say that it is the best place for them because Jesus said it was not.

Please note well that I do not mean to say that any scriptures referenced primarily have a symbolic meaning due to the applications I make of them. Some are indeed symbolic, but many have or will have a literal, illustrative fulfillment. I make use of them according to this divine principle embedded in the Word: "All scripture is given by inspiration of God, and is profitable for doctrine, for reproof, for correction, for instruction in righteousness: that the man of God may be perfect, througly furnished unto all good works."*

If you are ever in doubt about some piece of Scripture, ask yourself first if it has a literal meaning God seems to want us to respect. Then, establishing this, permit the Holy Spirit to use the scriptures—those little truths that comprise the whole Truth—as He will for the sake of your personal growth. We tend to limit God to what is merely what many like to refer to as its original context. This is always good to know if you can search it out, but it is not the whole of the Word, or why God left us with such a large Covenant-book. Most certainly underlying principles of the Word have been revealed to uneducated souls who were diligently seeking to understand God's ways though they had no opportunities to become educated (in the way this typically means to Man). They would not

---

* II Timothy 3:16-17

necessarily understand what is meant by context, but they very well may be able to illuminate the meaning of certain words far better than those who teach on their original context simply because they allowed the Holy Spirit to teach them.*

GOD always wants to provide good things for His children. By building up in His spiritual Kingdom these two mounts, He was not giving us a choice between something good and something bad. As we have spoken of before, the Mountain of Feeling is wonderful for vacationing on. There are many healthy recreations available to us there. But on the Mountain of Faith is much richer soil for the regular reaping and sowing of cyclical living, which will continue to be a necessary pattern for as long as the

---

* John 14:26—"But the Comforter (Counselor, Helper, Intercessor, Advocate, Strengthener, Standby), the Holy Spirit, Whom the Father will send in My name [in My place, to represent Me and act on My behalf], He will teach you all things. And He will cause you to recall (will remind you of, bring to your remembrance) everything I have told you" (AMPC).

earth endures, both physically and spiritually.* For God's part He purposed to provide two wonderful mountains to be a part of the landscape of the blessed life. And He graciously placed the Valley of Fact between them so that we would be reminded of where we are whenever we are shifting between one and the other. It is we who interpret God's purposes to be other than what they often are.

So consider this likeness: consider that a Portal is the means of our travel into the spiritual Kingdom of God. This vortex is the way by which we travel from the realm of the spiritually dead to the spiritually alive. This is why I say this is where the soul *lives*, because it is spiritually translated into the Land wherein everything is made alive.

---

* Genesis 8:22—"While the earth remaineth, seedtime and harvest, and cold and heat, and summer and winter, and day and night shall not cease." A cyclical pattern conforms to the principle of increments: things change in their season, and in large part we are not asked to take up the responsibilities of summer during winter. Life is divided into parts so that we may be better able to bear the fullness of its tasks. They also speak to us of God's principles, seedtime and harvest being one of the biggest principles in the Kingdom.

Now imagine emerging from this Portal—the Gate which is Christ—onto a great river, whose waters are crystal clear—clean and refreshing. These are the waters from the wells of salvation of which Jesus speaks.* These waters flow from within us because they originate in Christ's salvation for us. This is why there is a great river in that land and why it is one of the first things we see, because it is the River of Redemption. Imagine that there are soft sandy beaches on either side of the River, and the slope of the watery floor to the shore is gradual and easy to walk because God purposed it to be so for His children.

What God did not purpose was the immediate settling down of His people on these sandy shores. He did not intend they build their spiritual structures directly alongside the River as though this were the only place they had access to the water, or the only place they had access to in His Kingdom. Is it not written that these waters of salvation will be in our soul "like a spring

---

* John 7:37-38, a reference to Isaiah 12:3

of water, whose waters fail not"? They were meant to "satisfy thy soul in drought,"* where we are to be at work in these drought-afflicted lands to "build the old waste places"† of those glorious structures God built for Man but the enemy destroyed in his many attacks against us. We are not meant to hover beside the River (and the Gate) due to fear that if we walk out of sight of it, its saving power to us is lost. In a sense, we are to carry the Portal and the River it opens upon with us.

The soft, sandy shores were intended as an accompaniment to the waters of refreshment—for drinking, cleansing, and healing—and souls joyfully find that no amount of filth clouds or dirties either the water or the sand. Fresh fruit, wholesome and tasty breads, baked goods, savory treats, nuts, and herbs are all available as soon as the newcomers are ready to partake of them for their pre-climb strengthening, which are all the various healthful spiritual foods God

---

* Both quotes are from Isaiah 58:11.

† Verse 12

has provided us. Praise, gratitude, prayer, love for God and neighbor, etc. — these all feed the soul with healthy spiritual foods. These sands are warm, dry, and perfectly comfortable to every soul whether a softer or harder surface is preferred. And the sand does not stick to wet skin or fill one's shoes, because unless you prefer the feeling of remaining wet, you emerge from the waters dry.

Souls traveling from place to place in the Kingdom continually picnic on these sands. That is what they are for. So as they reminisce about their own first occasion there and of all the wonderful truths God has provided us, there are many souls present to greet newcomers. In this way the newcomers are embraced, and the old-timers are reminded of where they began and how they owe everything to the bounteous grace of our good God. And these do not need to be face-to-face conversations. We speak in a sense with the old-timers by listening to testimonies recorded long ago, in books and videos or by another soul relaying them to us. Yet in the spiritual it can be said that the life of the old-timer interacted with that of the newcomer, because something occurs in the spiritual that is greater than what happens in the natural. "…we also are compassed about with so great a cloud of witnesses…"*

And how do souls cross over between these two great mountains? Through the River. Traveling through the Valley of Fact and being refreshed by the Waters of Salvation is looked upon as nothing but a good thing by the old-timers. The more they make the journey, the more they are strengthened; and then the easier it becomes to move back and forth between the mountains. Those who cannot make the journey (or believe they are not strong enough for it) often become souls who emphasize faith over feeling or feeling over faith, and then they settle down on either side of the River in the shadow of one of the mounts. They are both a part of the Christ-life. It is just that one was designed for everyday living and the other for visiting

---

* Hebrews 12:1

and celebration and so forth. And both were designed to be lived *upon*, temporarily or permanently, not alongside and not under. As we sit in the heavenlies in Christ,[*] everything is under our feet, not merely the evil Jesus came to defeat. We are to stand above all things in Him, to use what we need when we need, and to be more than a conqueror in all.

That there are difficult emotions too, such as grief, takes us back to the enemy who is ever attempting to drag us back to his kingdom of death and destruction. We do not have to understand every last detail of the spiritual life to take some likeness of it. Just tuck away those likenesses you don't fully understand into the back of your note-book where you jot odd thoughts, and trust them to God. Often we are able to discern in greater detail later.

We were meant to find the Path up the Mount of Faith. That we can always feel, as we journey and live on this massive Rock, is common sense. Again, it is the founda-

---

[*] Ephesians 2:6

tion stone we choose to live on that is the distinction here, the ruling domain. For this reason the Path we take up this Mountain, the Path of Christ, the Way of our Salvation, is from certain angles all but indiscernible to the natural eye; but it *is* there, and there are signposts everywhere, as well as little side paths that take you this way and that (depending on where you are alongside the Mountain when you begin to go up it), which sooner or later intersect with this main Path. Remember, the Gate, or the Portal into the Kingdom, is our salvation. These little paths are not other ways to the main Way, as though I am trying to incorporate other religions into Christianity (which never works when one truly comprehends what the latter is all about); they are merely those little ways in which God steers us to a more concentrated following of the Way of Christ.

To make the choice easier between the Mountains when first setting out on the journey to establish a spiritual home, God made the path up the Mountain of Feeling indiscernible to those whose vision is still dulled by the dark kingdom they have just left. This is why countless souls feel no change at all when they first say a prayer of salvation, because God is trying to make it their first solid act of faith, and He uses it to strengthen their faith and sharpen their spiritual vision the first instant they step through the Gate. So most souls do begin — if they leave the sandy beaches — by clambering up the little paths on the Mount of Faith until they firmly locate the Path of Christ, and then they journey on from there.

And I refer to these little paths because the vast majority of believers are not proficient enough in matters of faith that their spiritual feet are firmly planted on the Way of Christ from the first moment. They combine a mixture of faith and feeling to fuel their spiritual life for a time, or it takes a few difficult trials before they realize they are not living by an abiding trust in the Saviour at all but by natural sight. Or they have erroneous lifestyle or philosophical tenets that they must leave off of and hold fast to Christ alone. These are the little paths to which I refer. If these souls continue on, they will be strengthened in their faith, and there will be no mistaking that they are walking, however imperfectly, the Path of Jesus. Or, finding the journey upward distasteful or overwhelming, they may turn around and settle down alongside the River. Regardless, you can see that in this allegory, all these still belong to the Kingdom. But those who dwell on the sand will never hold the same positions of authority in the Kingdom as do those who labor to climb the Mountain of Faith. They are awarded high places of authority because they aspired to climb higher in their faith in God.

Some newcomers insist on searching for a way up the Mountain of Feeling, but it is rare to find an easy path quickly. These are usually more adventurous ones whose souls have not been made subject yet to the rule of Christ, and they resent being kept from another way than one they have chosen for themselves. And since most souls begin to ascend the other Mount, it feeds their ego to take the road less traveled. They also can feel much strength of soul still (the fleshly kind), and so look upon the scaling of the steep sides of this Mount as a challenge. In short, they thoroughly resent being told they must by faith enter the Kingdom, because they much prefer feeling things. Nevertheless, they did enter by faith (for no matter how much feeling we have, we are still choosing to believe in a Man that is presently invisible to us, which is faith, pure and simple); and seeing a great mountain called Feeling, they cannot resist having a go at it immediately.

Occasionally there is an old-timer present who beckons the newcomer toward the path he found long ago to scale the Mount of Feeling, being one of those who decided to make his home there. Usually there are others to caution the newcomer that the Lord desires he first ascend the Mount of Faith, but as said, God will not violate our freedom of choice. The newcomer has the privilege of deciding to go with one — who is also of the Kingdom — who encourages scaling a steep path he long since discovered for himself on the Mount of Feeling, rather than receiving the word of what the Lord desires he do. If he decides to first scale the steeper path, in looking back I would say, if his soul has grown at all, he realizes that in that moment his sense of self was directing his course more than his spirit. The point is, there is still a wide variety of spiritual growth around us after we have entered the Kingdom, and our likenesses can reveal this. They do not have to all convey the spiritual perfection we will someday obtain. Let them reflect the idiosyncrasies of this in-between life too if they seem to take that course. Again, let the Holy Spirit consecrate your meditations.

Some wander around aimlessly for a time, accustomed to being so enveloped by their feeling but seeing no way up that Mount, which naturally strikes them as the most fitting for them, that they do not know how to proceed. They are ones not necessarily bound to do things their own way — many appear very humble — but they just don't know how to process things apart from their faculty of feeling. But there is no lack of cries of encouragement in this Land — though at times smallness of faith obscures fellow travelers from view—especially at and near the Gate where these sands are, so many soon find themselves on the lower slopes of the Mount of Faith and begin climbing alongside their fellows. And if these fellows are not revealed by their faith, then as I said, the paths up the Mount of Faith are much more discernible than on the Mount of Feeling, so they eventually just start up this one by default.

Remember that I likened the Mountain of Faith to the Appalachian Mountain chain on the east side of our varied states, and the Mountain of Feeling to the Rocky Mountain chain in the west in another letter?[*] The latter has peaks several times taller than most of those in the east, and its climate is much more arid, making growing plants much more difficult. Liken this to the nurturing of spiritual fruits on the spiritual Mounts.

God desires that we make it as swiftly as is safe to the place that is good ground for our home of faith—that place where we are

---

[*] I refer to *An Epistle on Judgment.*

settled and secure in our ability to live with what is presently for us largely an invisible reality — and no matter how much of the spiritual we may see while still here, they are but glimpses until we make it Home to dwell in the Father's heavenly Kingdom. It is here in our little spiritual abode that we commune with God in our spirit. Some believe we can do this through feeling, and we certainly do still have access to the faculty of feeling while living in the domain of Faith. It is just that our spiritual structure is much better fashioned from the living stones of our faith. If it helps, think of it very basically, such as in the tale of the three little pigs: foolish ones build of straw and wood; wise ones build of brick and stone; and there are always wolves seeking to devour us. And there will always be a wiser Brother among us to Whom we can run for sanctuary. Just add to this that the wise pig built his home on the Mountain of Faith.

So we have access to feeling anywhere in God's Kingdom because everything that exists there is of His Kingdom. But the creation of the inner portal that is our conduit between God's Spirit and ours—this can only be created on the Mountain of Faith because it is faith which is the natural force (spiritually speaking) which enables the connection. We had access to the original Portal because we entered through the Gate which is Christ, and this primary access is meant to get us up the Mountain of Faith until we get our soul established in God. This being an inner portal, which is only created through the faculty of free will, we then take it with us wherever we go. (—or *connected* to God, rather than created; you can look at it as the portal being in place in all souls, but some never have it connected to God.) This is why I tell you to make it back to the Path on the Mountain of Faith if you get turned around (as we all do from time to time in this shadowland), because this Rock is our Cornerstone. It is here that we build and maintain a dwelling on a foundation God long since built for us: "Now therefore ye are no more strangers and foreigners, but fellowcitizens with the saints, and of the household of God; and are built upon the foundation of the apostles and prophets, Jesus Christ Himself being the chief corner stone; in whom all the building fitly framed together groweth unto an holy temple in the Lord: in whom ye also are builded together for an habitation of God through the Spirit."* The Mount of Faith is the soul's cornerstone, but the cornerstone comprises just a portion of the great structure. And remember, the whole Kingdom is in Christ, so the soul does not leave Him behind when it visits the Mount of Feeling. But I barely touch upon here the great truths encapsulated in these few verses.

Every virtue has a mountain in the Kingdom of God, and you will find counterparts too of the mountain peaks of culture, those some refer to as the mountains of influence. They exist here on earth because they first exist There in God's Kingdom. We do not find corruption at their peaks because the mountains themselves were creations of the enemy. The enemy can only counterfeit what God has created. So do not limit what

* Ephesians 2:19-22

God can reveal through likenesses. They are great substances for fueling our contemplations and nurturing our faith. If anything seems amiss in your inner pictures, just toss them away and ask God for new ones. They ought not be so special to us or vital to our faith that we cannot start over at any time. It is Jesus Christ and Him crucified* that we must not let go of.

The Way to Life is narrow and many fail to perceive it.† But once in the Way, the land opens up broadly—widely, deeply, and longly. It is hidden space. Are there not many stories of hidden spaces? What of the wardrobe that led to Narnia?‡ I tell you the truth, there is nothing envisioned by Man for which there does not exist some heavenly counterpart that is exponentially greater. They may not always take just the form or scope we imagine they would, but I tell you, they are *better*.

---

* I Corinthians 2:2

† Matthew 7:13-14

‡ *The Lion, the Witch, & the Wardrobe* of the Chronicles of Narnia by C.S. Lewis.

Again—and I cannot stress this enough—the point is the *foundational* nature of the two Mountains, the ruling domain. The soul must choose, of its own free will, on which Mount to make its spiritual home, or to settle in the Valley of Fact.

From the Mountain of Faith, the whole Kingdom is opened to the soul, because it has everything it needs in its little abode on that Mount. It has access through the moving portal for whatever it needs to live or to travel back down the Mountain into the Valley and up the Mountain of Feeling or any other mountain of virtue or influence or contour in the spiritual land.

If the soul chooses to make its spiritual home on the Mountain of Feeling, it will spend much of its time laboring to pull together a basic spiritual sustenance, for the climate there is arid, as it is in those western mountains I mentioned. No matter how rich the experiences feel there—these are weather systems that move in and out—the climate itself is arid, and growing fruits and other crops there is a hard task.

If the soul chooses to settle itself comfortably in the Valley of Fact, it makes itself vulnerable to rockslides and flash floods, as we have discussed in another letter.*

Once fully translated, nothing in the Kingdom will be able to harm us. The soul will be made of the Christ-mettle, which can withstand the strength and the fire of the Living God and the substance of all He has created. It is only while we are here, as we know in part and receive the Christ-life in increments so God can never be accused of having coerced us to receive that which we did not wish to receive, that we have to exercise good judgment in where to settle the soul. Presently we live in part There and in part here, though we are obliged to follow the principles set down for us from There. This is why we are fools to the world, because the world cannot comprehend why, when its ways provide so much wisdom for getting ahead, we reject its standard and hold fast instead to a standard based on an invisible reality. We know we

---

* I refer to *An Epistle to the Moderately Miserable.*

do this because we trust God keeps good account books for us, and He will see that we are adequately compensated for whatever we do to serve Him. But to the world, God is not real, not in that everyday sense that we live with. Souls sincerely love Him, but many do not believe we can truly know Him; and it is this effort at great devotion they do not understand. Keep climbing. The effort is worth it.

PLEASE note as you read these things that there *is* a real Kingdom of God in Heaven, and this is why we pray Thy Kingdom come in earth just as it is in Heaven.* But while still on earth, we access God's Kingdom spiritually. Some visit it so clearly in their spirit that they see it largely as it exists in that land far away. But some perceive its likenesses. I am speaking to you of likenesses. Though I believe we can learn a tremendous amount about spiritual life and a childlike state of faith from accounts of

---

* Matthew 6:10; Luke 11:2

Heaven some bring us, God's principles—
our principal focus—are often better
described through the use of likenesses, I
believe, and here I explain why—

Someday God will bring all creation into
a seamless whole, the material and the spiritual, as He first created it all to be, but presently we live with the symbolic outlines of
spiritual shapes.

I fully believe God would be pleased
with many more souls able to step into
Heaven to visit while still living here, and
we should embrace the knowledge we are
given by seasoned seers of God. Why some
Christian leaders teach this is wrong, or the
seers are wrong to believe they are visiting
Heaven, eludes me (or they expressly declare that people do not visit Heaven), for
did the Lord not say, "*As in Heaven, so on the
earth*"? How are we to know what earth
should be like if no one of us ever sees a bit
of Heaven? And more than one prophetic
voice in the Bible did so. So either God, as
many say, no longer does things as He once
did, even though we are promised Jesus is

the same yesterday, today, and forever,* the same Jesus who appeared to John and of Whom he declared, "The Revelation of Jesus Christ, which God gave unto him, to shew unto His servants things which must shortly come to pass"† — or they are in effect saying we ought to discount what is revealed in God's Word.

Also, I am not sure God will completely dispense with these symbolic likenesses before He catches His Church away from this earth, because it is in the likenesses that we must exercise our faith. And God requires the exercising of our faith in order to demonstrate that He is not coercing us to follow Him. We follow Him because we have chosen of our own free will to seek Him out. We are not seeking out what is always right in front of our eyes. That is like saying we chose to eat lots of fruits and vegetables and other nutritious foods of our own free will when someone else provided all our groceries for us and it was just at

---

* Hebrews 13:8
† Revelation 1:1

hand. Would we have chosen to buy all those healthy items if we had come across them in the store? How would we or anyone else know what we would have chosen? It would not be a real test of our convictions were the evidences of our faith set before us. Jesus told Thomas frankly, "Blessed are they that have not seen, and yet have believed."* It is what we are willing to exchange for the pearl of great price that counts.†

It is difficult to express just where the line between the spiritual and the natural is. The more one lives in the spiritual, the more natural it all becomes, and then the natural begins to take on a shadow appearance. No longer does it hold the substance it once did. When one is first beginning to take likenesses, it is best not to become frustrated trying to make every little detail analogous to something in the natural, be-

---

* John 20:29
† Matthew 13:45-46; and in vv. 44-48, Jesus takes three likenesses, all of the Kingdom of Heaven. So we are never limited to just one. Many different things reflect the truths we live by.

cause there is much overlap between the two realms—because that is how they were created to be in the beginning. It can seem like a jumbled mess because the lenses of world, flesh, and devil obscure our vision, and all these sights get mingled with the heavenly ones. God sees it all clearly, though, so just trust Him to steer you back onto the Path when you get distracted by some little aspect you don't understand. Just keep in mind that the spiritual and the natural are not as separated as we tend to believe.

The substance of these spiritual shapes is greater than their material counterparts, though it can feel just the opposite to us. This is why we speak in parables, because the invisible is given likeness in what we have touched, seen, and heard in the flesh. This whole earth and its various parts and creations were designed to reflect the invisible, greater reality of God's spiritual Kingdom. It is not invisible to those who are There; it is invisible to the souls who walk the earth. And this is why the earth was made in likeness to the spiritual realm—so that by faith we might take hold of what is of greater substance than what we touch, see, hear, taste, and feel. These faculties were given to us in part so that through them the spiritual is given likeness for our greater understanding, and so that there will be a record that of our own free will we either received them or rejected them. Again, one does not immediately have to fully understand what one chooses to respect, just as a little child may not comprehend the sun and stars in the sky but it chooses to accept the word it has been given that this is what they are.

So if we cannot receive God's truths through parables, then we reveal an inability to receive His Truth at all (at least at that time), because there are no simpler likenesses to affix to these spiritual truths for our understanding if the ones we have seen, felt, and heard have failed us.

Jesus did not speak in parables to exclude some souls from understanding: He spoke in parables because it was the best way to describe the nature of the spiritual realm and how it works. We focus on

Matthew 13:13-15, and yet many of us tend to completely overlook verse 35: "I will open My mouth in parables; I will utter things which have been kept secret from the foundation of the world."

Parables *reveal* hidden things; they were not used by God to further obscure the spiritual realm. They utilize what the people have seen and heard and felt in the physical because these things are, well, natural to them. But this natural seeing and hearing did not help them at all when Jesus told them His little stories. So, "though seeing, they do not see..."* And thus are fulfilled Jesus' words of verses 14-15 too.

There was no more He could say that they would have been able to understand if they could not understand His meaning through what was already completely natural to their lives. The best frame of reference He could give them was essentially lost on them. It would have done no good to rephrase His teachings because there were no simpler terms to use. They could

---

* Matthew 13:13

not understand them because they had fostered no appreciation for the secret things of God. God did not make them the fulfillment of this prophecy: He simply knew there would be some at the time of His Son's visitation to this earth who would fulfill it. For His part He was laboring to reveal things that had remained hidden for eons. "All these things spake Jesus unto the multitude in parables; and without a parable spake He not unto them."*

SO ALL this inner land is Christ. This is our Truth: He is the River of our Redemption. He is our Path in the spiritual life, and our Way of Salvation to God. He is the Rock upon which we establish our life. The inner land is all Jesus. *It is all the same Rock no matter which part of the ground the soul is walking over.* We live upon It, and It—the spiritual Rock—moves with us as we move

---

* Matthew 13:34

about in the natural realm.* No matter what emotional state we may be in, or what the outward circumstances of our life are, the Rock follows us; so we can always reach the little abode of faith we helped build on this Rock. For it is written that nothing shall separate us from the love of Christ.†

Though the outward appearance of the rock of the Mountain of Faith may differ from that in the Valley and the other Mountain, it is all of the same foundational Rock which is Christ. The outward is often the attribute we see this side of the veil so that we are enabled to discern with better understanding, such as love, integrity, devotion, etc.

The rock on the Mountain of Faith may appear as sedimentary. The rock on the Mountain of Feeling as either granite or some sparkling gem — or many sparkling gems encrusted together on a surface of silver and gold. (There are even more gold

---

* I Corinthians 10:4—"And did all drink the same spiritual drink: for they drank of that spiritual Rock that followed them: and that Rock was Christ."
† Romans 8:38-39

and silver and gems running through the Mountain of Faith, but they are hidden deep below the surface, and only God reveals the entrances to them to those who ask and who walk blamelessly before Him.) The rock of the Valley may take the form of innumerable small pebbles worn smooth by the waters — giving likeness to the multitude of truths we have been so graciously given to live by, their rough edges of brutal honesty regarding the soul's tendency toward sin softened by the healing content of Christ's Spirit, our spiritual water of life. Even the sand is the material of rock ground down until the pieces are miniscule and soft, perhaps giving likeness to the way in which Jesus' body and soul were continuously assaulted by the evils of this world — and those He loved who rejected Him — and this soft, yielding sand for our comfort was what was produced from it.

Yes, all the underlying rock is Christ, whether on mountain or on sand, and you can see how it is not a matter of some being good and some being bad. Even so, from Jesus' instruction, it is still not wise to build a house on sand. The ultimate reflection of this truth is to choose to build apart from the Rock of Redemption, but we are free to pursue unwise choices in the Kingdom as well. And the principle of the natural, as said, is the reflection of the spiritual law. So even in the Kingdom, sand is not the best place on which to build a home of faith. Its purposes are devoted to other things.

The different forms of rock (and all the varied contours of the inner land) have different purposes, which all together form the blessed life. We have the freedom to move about the inner land as we will, though God asks us to be ready to submit to His will at all times, for those times when our will may be in conflict with His. What I highlight to you in many letters is the soul's need to live on the Mountain of Faith. Embrace the ongoing spiritual travels of this journey involving the interior life. But when you return to your abode, your little place in Christ where you find quiet and refreshment for your soul, make sure you are back on the Mountain of Faith.

If I was not fully clear, I earnestly believe some souls do see beyond the veil and visit Heaven. Again, I do not understand why some Christians say visiting Heaven is not what God allows or that God does not want us focusing on Heaven, as though this means we are focused on death and dying. How could this possibly be? Heaven is the abode of eternal *LIFE*. The only depictions of death you will find there are the monuments of Christ's cross and the bronze serpent on the pole. Moreover, Paul stated without prevarication, "For to me to live is Christ, and to die is gain."* We must have some likeness of Heaven if we are to comprehend what this life in the natural is all about, since the visible gives image to the invisible, and the invisible heavenly operates according to the will of God. Also, this earthly life is but the seed of the soul's everlasting life. It is common sense that we ought to be able to appreciate a little bit of what we are working toward.

---

* Philippians 1:21

I believe Jesus spoke in likenesses not simply because the people's spiritual vision had grown so dull they could not comprehend anything but the simplest language. He spoke His meanings through likenesses because they were so miserable in soul they could not have borne a greater revelation of heavenly things and then persevered through that tumultuous transition into the Church Age. They would have wanted to immediately give up the ghost and leave the earth to the violent and wicked when the first wave of persecution began.

And are we not enduring a similar transition now—from the Church Age to the Kingdom Age? And have we not established that the way the Kingdom of God works on earth is based on how it works in Heaven? The principles are the same. The earthly reflects the heavenly. It is not the image reflected that contains the substance; it is the object for which the glass produced an image which has all the substance. We must come to a better understanding of Heaven if we are to comprehend to any useful degree how the Kingdom of God ought to work in this earth. And to know where our loved ones are and some of what they are about after having left us is, of course, comforting.

Remember that we have committed to praying for the Church to become strong in knowledge of God and in the practice of His spiritual principles. This is why we discuss these things—because God bids us pray into His people the strengthening that comes from being a people of principles. There are greater principles than just moral or financial ones. Good principles are always based on the spiritual ones that exist in Heaven, and which God implanted in this earth upon its creation. Think of them too as part of our quantum reality.

Too long has the Church spiritually existed by the tossing of emotional waves. Too long has it made excuse about everything being relative so its members could live however they desired. Experiences are individual, regardless that we can glean much knowledge from them. The whole point in taking likenesses is to better perceive divine principles at work, to better perceive the general standard God set for Man. As we see our hope made manifest — strong principles, strong Body — God will demonstrate that our spiritual labors were not in vain.

If you desire to see more of God's likenesses, as for them. If you desire to see Heaven itself, ask Him how to do that. The point is not to limit Him either way. He can use likenesses such as the ones I have given you in my letters, and He can use the direct experience of visiting the real thing. He likes to use both. Which He uses at a given time is a complex matter, the solution to one of those equations too complex most of the time for us to compute. So be open to both, trust Him, and remember that He gives grace to endure all things — whether it be visiting Heaven and having to return here, or having to be patient with practicing in likenesses when you would really rather have a few direct sights of what is usually invisible.

If you receive heavenly visions, test the spirit of them. If they *bear the likeness* [smile of irony] of the God who is Love but also

Just, True, Pure, etc., and do not contradict His Word, then receive them. But if you do not receive visions yet you are persisting in your labors of prayer for the Church's healing and growth, keep this word in mind: "Greater love hath no man than this, that a man lay down his life for his friends."* *Nothing* we do for the sake of the Church out of Christ's love for her falls void. The soul which sacrifices its self for the well-being of those Jesus loves is as the man who lays down his life for his friends, just as the Lord did for us. His sacrifice was once for all; ours is most often in increments — in those moments when we are faced with either feeding the self or sacrificing in some way to be able to remain in the prayer closet.

God can see how much you are laying down to have fulfilled in you the purposes for which He sent you into this earth, and He has it all entered into the chronicle of your life. Do not concern yourself with what any other soul is seeing beyond the

---

* John 15:13

veil (i.e., do not concern yourself by the thought you are receiving less revelation), only test those visions too and receive them gladly as though God sent them directly to you. For this is why He told them to share the visions with us—because He wants us to receive in some measure what another has received. This is what it means to be a *Body*. Does the stomach consume food to its satisfaction yet not share it with the arms and legs which lift and walk? So also are we entitled to a share for our well-being of that which was given to another. Again, let the Holy Spirit guide. But in this way your soul will be comforted, but the weight and possible grief of those sights will be softened and better able for your soul to bear. (The soul can feel grief after viewing such sights and being required to remain here, for not every soul wishes to remain here unto a great length of days. There are actually a few here and there—wonder of wonders— whose hearts hold close a longing to be released from this land of sin and self. Heaven is not a place to them for those who have died; it is a Place for those who live in greater measure than they ever have before.)

The weight of spiritual substance far exceeds that of the physical. You feel the burden of the spiritual because there really is a heavy burden while we must persist in this weak earthly frame. It isn't referred to the weight of His glory for no reason. The burden gradually lightens as self is increasingly transformed into the likeness of Christ. And always, in Christ we can do all things by His strength.* So through Him or with Him, we are covered.

Remember to take your rest as you need, whenever you sense your soul leaning toward misery or resentment or some other negative state. Reading or watching some light entertainment is a fully acceptable activity—God loves a good story, or Jesus would not have told so many—just take the time for a short devotion first when such a state is pressing upon you. I find it helpful to have several brief daily devotionals, one here and one there, so that they are at hand

---

* Philippians 4:13

throughout the day when my soul needs help raising its gaze to higher things. Or I inch my way through some worthy tome a few pages at a time. Perhaps you will find this helpful too. The principle is to not let too many hours pass without raising your gaze toward God. Remember that the church bells once rung throughout the day not just to keep track of time before the advent of clocks, but to recall the people to thoughts of the heavenly. And be mindful of which recreations flatten your soul, so to speak, and which do not. When you sense something flattens your soul — makes it feel as if its connection to God has a kink in it like in a garden hose — avoid that recreation whenever possible. The Spirit is saying that activity or that kind of recreation is not for you. Go sit with the Lord for a few minutes and ask Him to fix the connection.

The key point in all this is that the boundaries between Faith and Feeling ought to be strong while we are still occupying the Kingdom realm in earth until our Lord returns. All this inner land is in Christ, but we do not grow into strong inner manhood without the proper exercise that patrols the borders — both against invaders from outside, but also against unwise travel within.

All praise to the One who reveals these great sights to our poor souls, which are spiritually wealthy only because we have Him. The grace of the Father, the loving sacrifice of the Son, and the presence of the Holy Spirit be with you always. In Jesus' Name, amen.